MELODY
Worrisome Heart
GARDOT

I need a hand with my worrisome heart...

Artwork and Photography:
© 2008 The Verve Music Group,
a Division of UMG Recordings, Inc.

 Alfred

Alfred Publishing Co., Inc.
16320 Roscoe Blvd., Suite 100
P.O. Box 10003
Van Nuys, CA 91410-0003
alfred.com

ISBN-10: 0-7390-5741-3
ISBN-13: 978-0-7390-5741-4

Contents

WORRISOME HEART

Words and Music by
MELODY GARDOT

6

Verses 1 & 2:

1. I_____ need a   hand   with my wor-ri-some_ heart._____
(2.) break   from my trou-bl-in'___ ways._____

I_____ need a   hand_____
I_____ need a   break_____

_____with my wor-ri-some_ heart._____   I would be luck-
_____from my trou-bl-in' ways._____   I would be luck-

who could love me the way that I am,_____ a

wor-ri - some,__ trou-bl - in',__ bag-gage-free__ mod-ern - day__ dame,_____

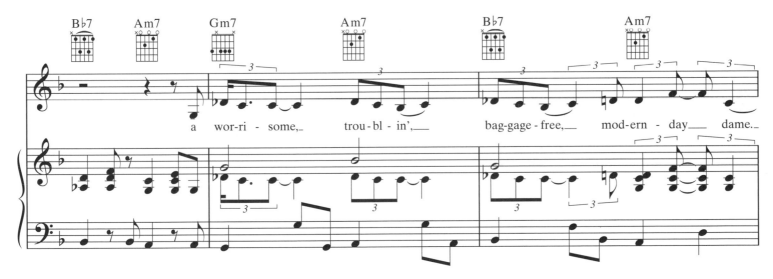

a wor-ri - some,__ trou-bl - in',__ bag-gage-free,__ mod-ern-day__ dame.__

Ain't no - bod - y the same.____

ALL THAT I NEED IS LOVE

Words and Music by
MELODY GARDOT

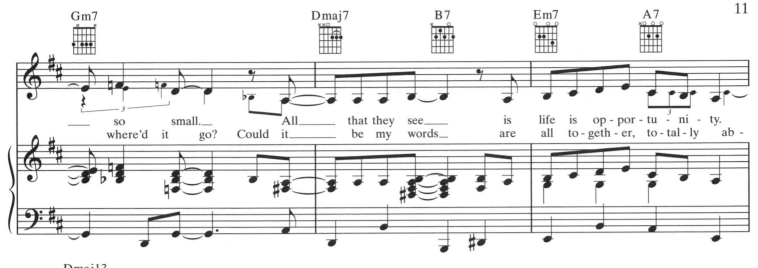

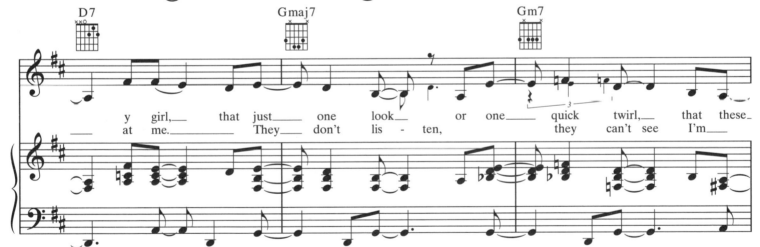

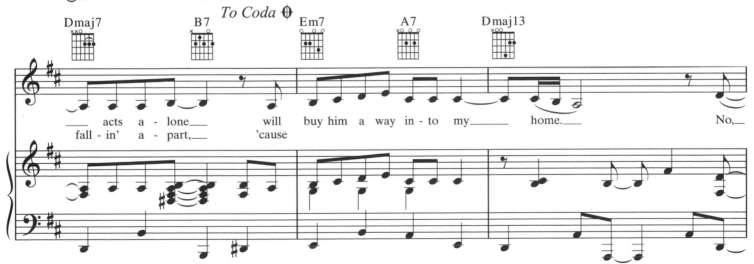

12

Verse 3:

GONE

Words and Music by
MELODY GARDOT

Gone - 6 - 1
31932

Verse 3:

3. I_____ won't have words;_____ I've said all that there is_____ to say._____ I_____ won't have_____ words,_____ 'cause I know you'll just throw_ them a - way._____ I_____

SWEET MEMORY

Words and Music by
MELODY GARDOT

Moderate blues shuffle ♩ = 108

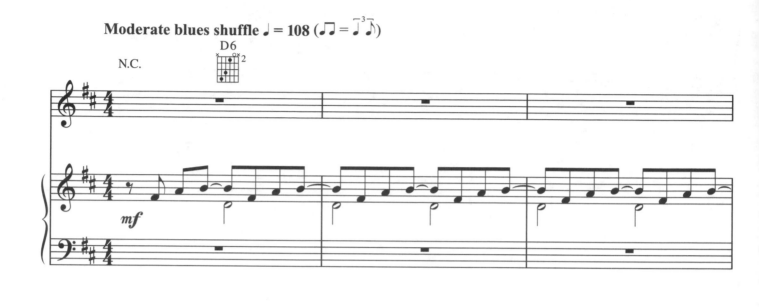

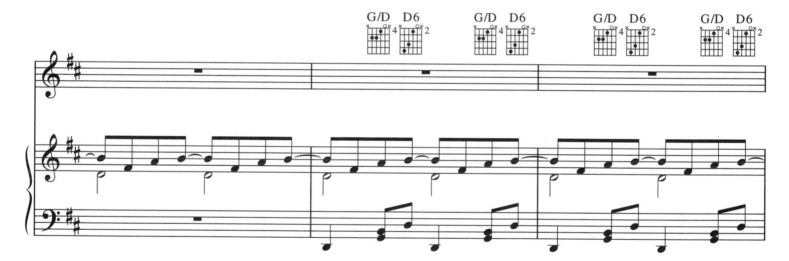

Mm.

§ *Verses 1 & 4:*

1.4. Sweet_____ mem - o - ry,_____

talk - in' 'bout a sweet_____ mem - o - ry._____

{ It goes 'round____ and 'round in my head.
  It goes 'round and 'round in my head._____

Pret-ty soon, I'll want the real thing in - stead,___ but for now,__ I got this

To Coda ⊕

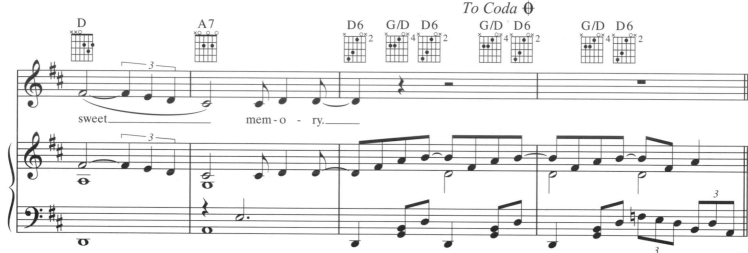

sweet___ mem - o - ry.___

Verses 2 & 3:

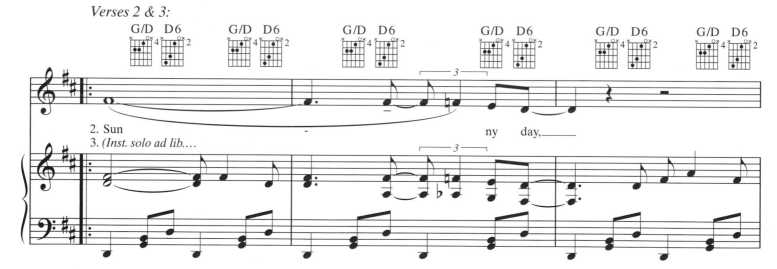

2. Sun - ny day,___
3. (Inst. solo ad lib....

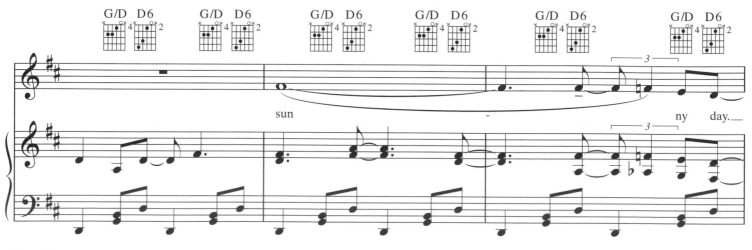

sun - ny day.___

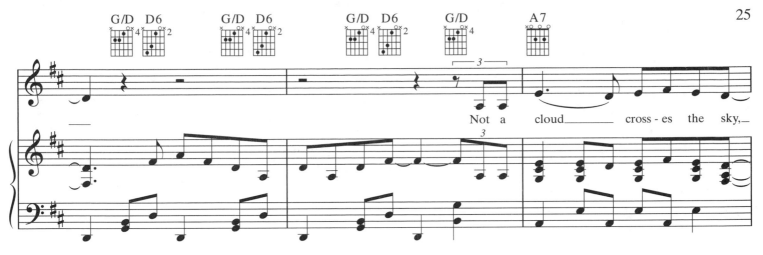

Not a cloud____ cross- es the sky,____

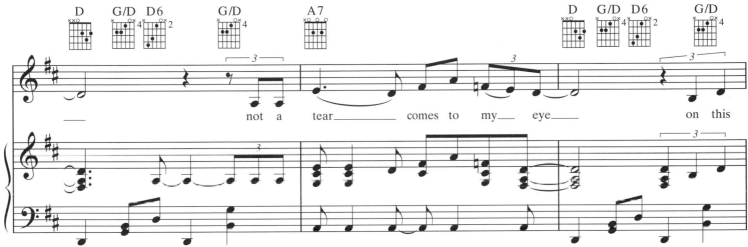

not a tear____ comes to my__ eye____ on this

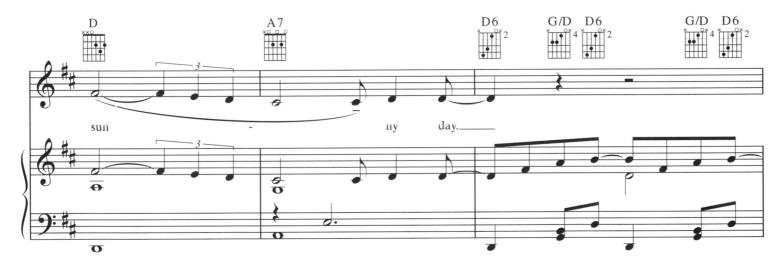

sun - ny day.____

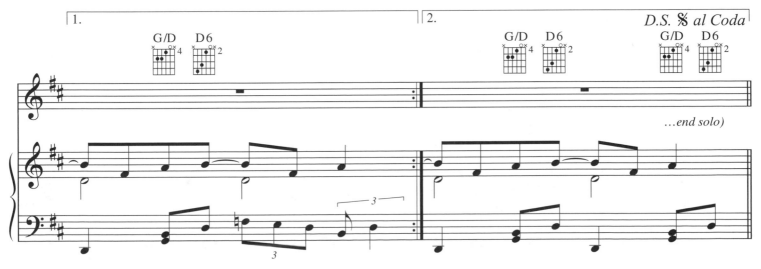

1.

2.

D.S. 𝄋 al Coda

...end solo)

SOME LESSONS

Words and Music by
MELODY GARDOT

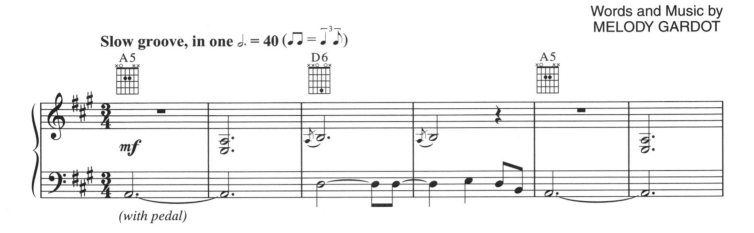

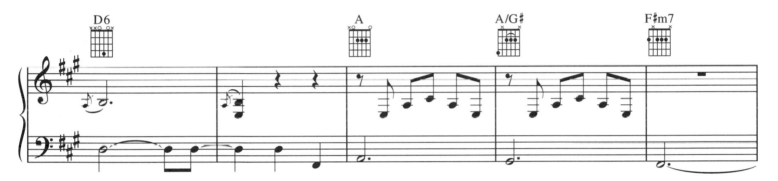

Ho,

Some Lessons - 8 - 1
31932

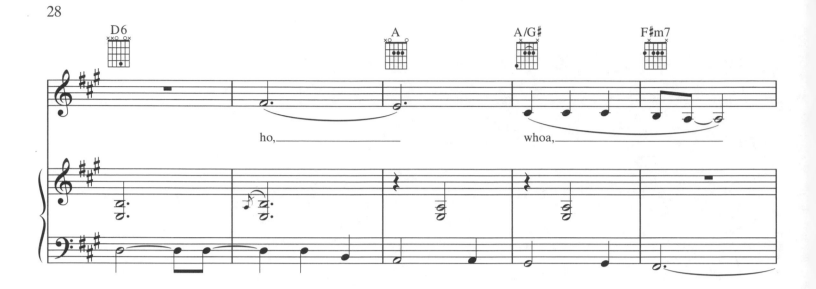

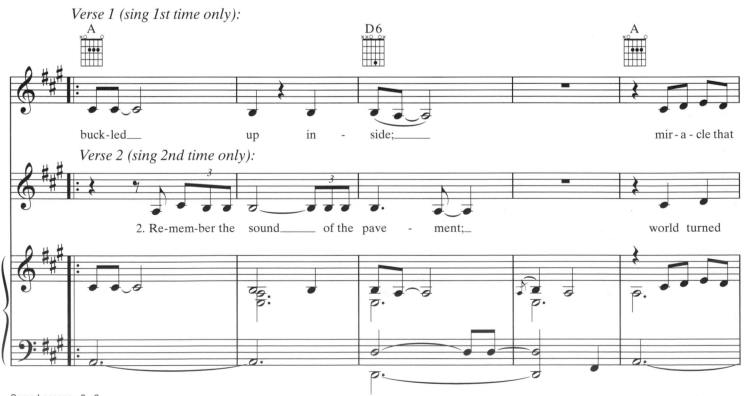

Verse 1 (sing 1st time only):

Verse 2 (sing 2nd time only):

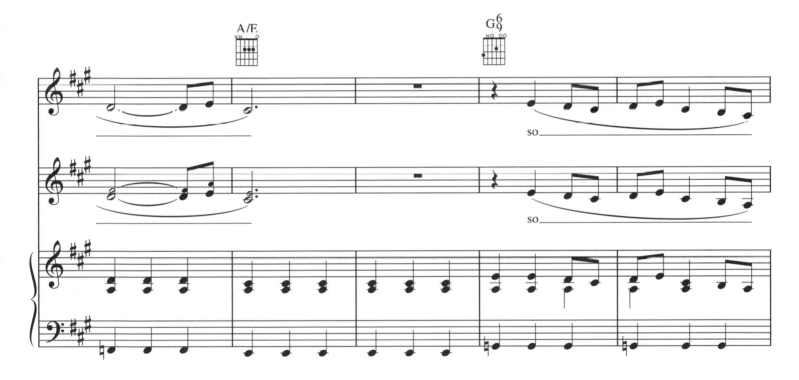

Chorus:

QUIET FIRE

Words and Music by
MELODY GARDOT

Moderately slow, easy groove ♩ = 100

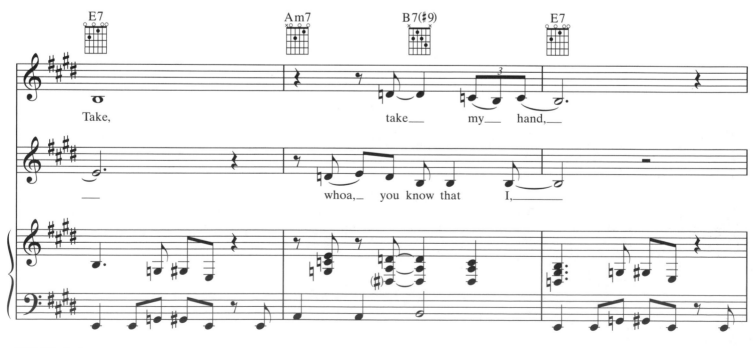

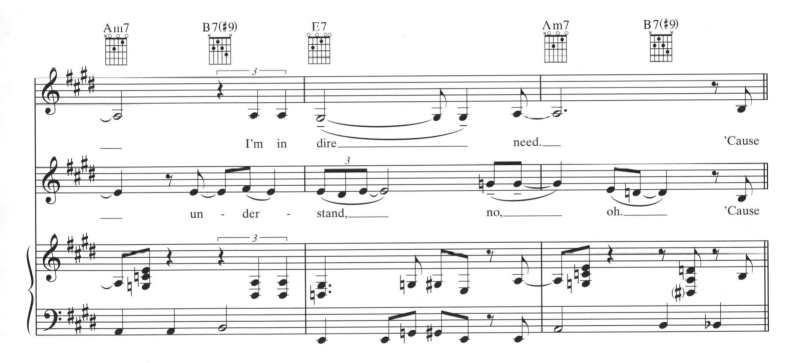

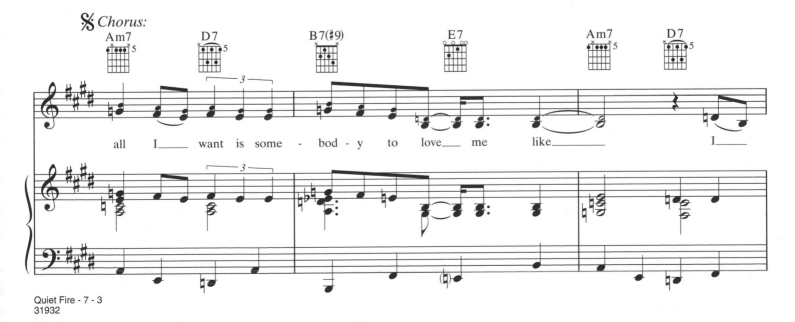

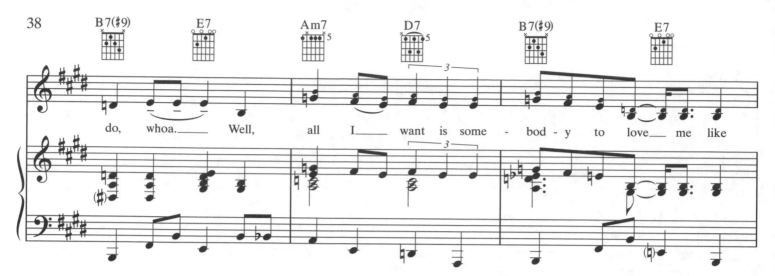

do, whoa._____ Well, all I_____ want is some - bod - y to love___ me like

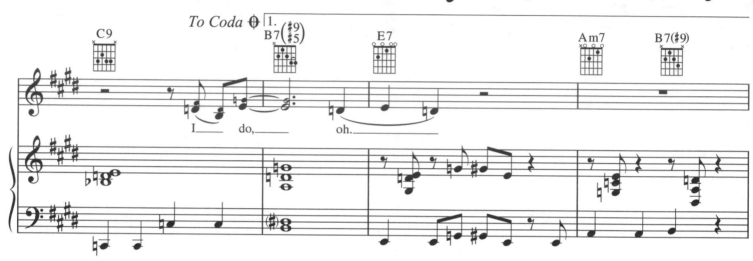

To Coda

I_____ do,_____ oh._____

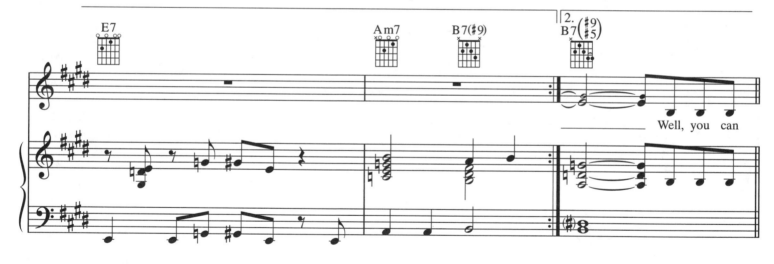

Well, you can

Bridge:

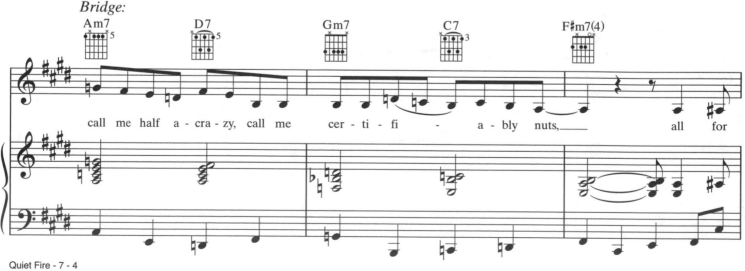

call me half a - cra - zy, call me cer - ti - fi - - a - bly nuts,_____ all for

love._____ What__ do you get for__ let - tin' me__ win__ so eas - 'ly?__

__ Put up your dukes, ba - by;__ what are ya made of? This is - n't right,__ no,

this is - n't right._____ You know that I'm not one to fuss, but a -

what have you done to me? You hard - ly make love__ to me now.__ Oh,__ my poor__

ONE DAY

Words and Music by
MELODY GARDOT

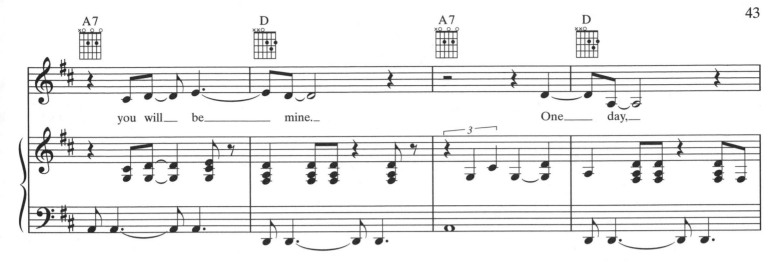

you will__ be_____ mine.__ One____ day,__

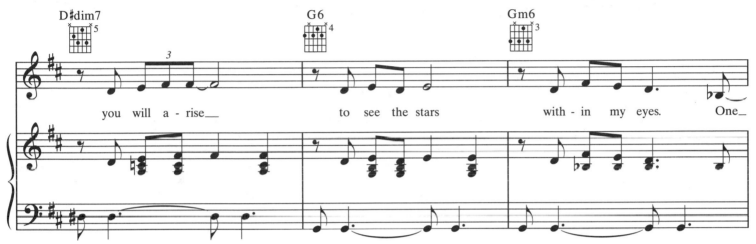

you will a - rise__ to see the stars with - in my eyes. One__

__ day, you will__ be_____ mine.__

Bridge:

(Trumpet)

One Day - 3 - 2
31932

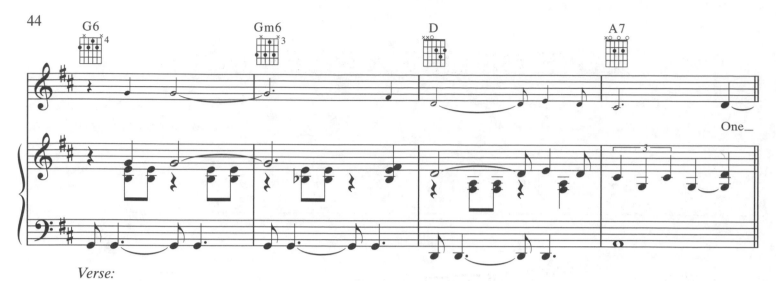

One___

Verse:

___ day,___ you will be mine. The clouds___ will part,___

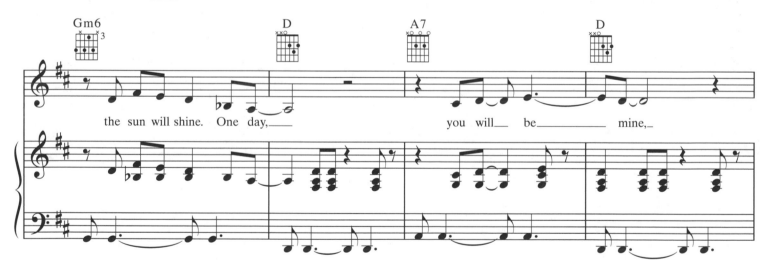

the sun will shine. One day,___ you will___ be___ mine,___

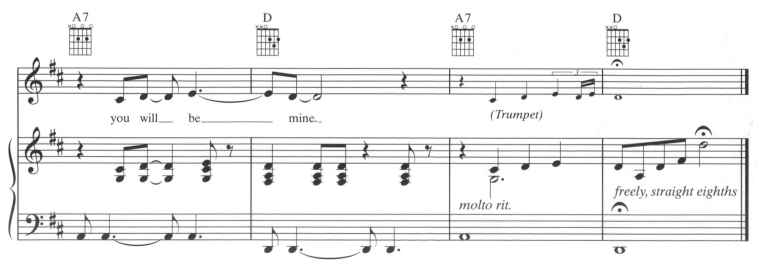

you will___ be___ mine.___ *(Trumpet)*

molto rit.

freely, straight eighths

LOVE ME LIKE A RIVER DOES

Words and Music by
MELODY GARDOT

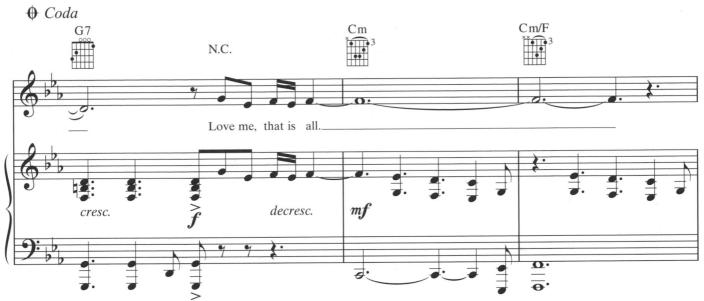

Love me, that is all._____

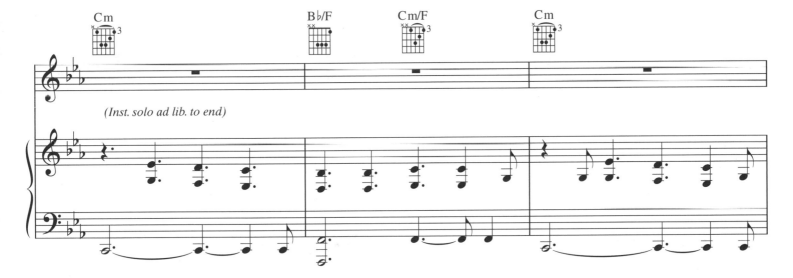

(Inst. solo ad lib. to end)

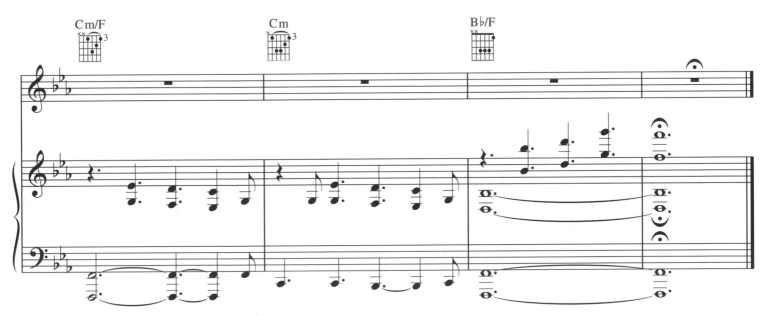

GOODNITE

Words and Music by
MELODY GARDOT

52

Chorus:

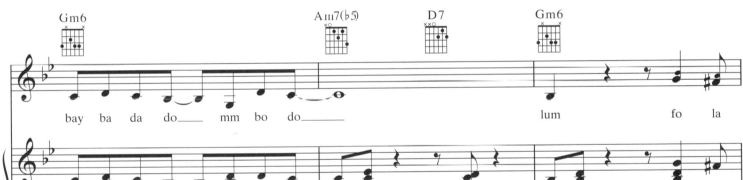

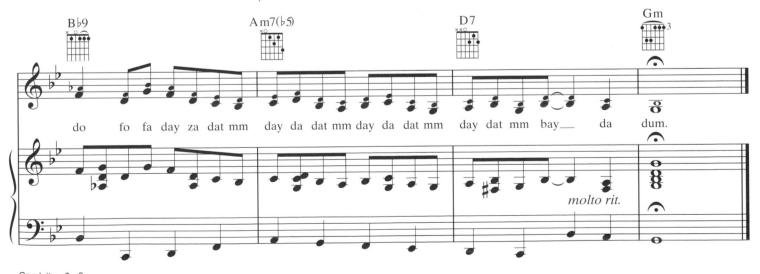